THE ANTITHETICAL MEANING
OF PRIMAL WORDS

BY

SIGMUND FREUD

British Library Cataloguing-in-Publication Data
A catalogue record for this book is available from the
British Library

Contents

Sigmund Freud

Sigismund Schlomo Freud was born on 6th May 1856, in the Moravian town of Příbor, now part of the Czech Republic.

Sigmund was the eldest of eight children to Jewish Galician parents, Jacob and Amalia Freud. After Freud's father lost his business as a result of the Panic of 1857, the family were forced to move to Leipzig and then Vienna to avoid poverty. It was in Vienna that the nine-year-old Sigmund enrolled at the Leopoldstädter Kommunal-Realgymnasium before beginning his medical training at the University of Vienna in 1873, at the age of just 17. He studied a variety of subjects, including philosophy, physiology, and zoology, graduating with an MD in 1881.

The following year, Freud began his medical career in Theodor Meynert's psychiatric clinic at the Vienna General Hospital. He worked there until 1886 when he set up in private practice and began specialising in "nervous disorders". In the same year he married Merth Bernays, with whom he had 6 children between 1887 and 1895.

In the period between 1896 and 1901, Freud isolated himself from his colleagues and began work on developing the basics of his psychoanalytic theory. He published *The Interpretation of Dreams*, in 1899, to a lacklustre reception, but continued to produce works such as *The Psychopathology of Everyday Life* (1901) and *Three Essays on the Theory of Sexuality* (1905). He held a weekly meeting at his home known as the "Wednesday Psychological Society" which eventually developed into the Vienna Psycho-Analytic Society. His ideas gained momentum and by the end of the decade his methods were being used internationally by neurologists and psychiatrists.

Freud made a huge and lasting contribution to the field of psychology with many of his methods still being used in modern psychoanalysis. He inspired much discussion on the wealth of theories he produced and the reactions to his works began a century of great psychological investigation.

In 1930 Freud fled Vienna due to rise of Nazism and resided in England until his death from mouth cancer on 23rd September 1939.

THE ANTITHETICAL MEANING OF PRIMAL WORDS (1910E)

In my *Interpretation of Dreams* I made a statement about one of the findings of my analytic work which I did not then understand. I will repeat it here by way of preface to this review:

'The way in which dreams treat the category of contraries and contradictories is highly remarkable. It is simply disregarded. "No" seems not to exist so far as dreams are concerned. They show a particular preference for combining contraries into a unity or for representing them as one and the same thing. Dreams feel themselves at liberty, moreover, to represent any element by its wishful contrary; so that there is no way of deciding at a first glance whether any element that admits of a contrary is present in the dream-thoughts as a positive or as a negative.'[1]

The dream-interpreters of antiquity seem to have made the most extensive use of the notion that a thing in a dream can mean its opposite. This possibility has also occasionally been recognized by modern students of dreams, in so far as they concede at all that dreams have a meaning and can be interpreted.[2] Nor do I think that I shall be contradicted if I assume that all who have followed me in interpreting dreams on scientific lines have found confirmation of the statement quoted above.

I did not succeed in understanding the dream-work's singular tendency to disregard negation and to employ the same means of representation for expressing contraries until I happened by chance to read a work by the philologist Karl Abel, which was published in 1884 as a separate pamphlet and included in the following year in the author's *Sprachwissenschaftliche Abhandlungen* [Philological Essays]. The subject is of sufficient interest to justify my quoting here the full text of the crucial passages in Abel's paper (omitting, however, most of the examples). We obtain from them the astonishing information that the behaviour of the dream-work which I have just described is identical with a peculiarity in the oldest languages known to us.

¹ *The Interpretation of Dreams* (1900*a*), p.787

² Cf. G. H. von Schubert (1814, Chapter II).

After stressing the antiquity of the Egyptian language which must have been developed a very long time before the first hieroglyphic inscriptions, Abel goes on (1884, 4):

'Now in the Egyptian language, this sole relic of a primitive world, there are a fair number of words with two meanings, one of which is the exact opposite of the other. Let us suppose, if such an obvious piece of nonsense can be imagined, that in German the word "strong" meant both "strong" and "weak"; that in Berlin the noun "light" was used to mean both "light" and "darkness"; that one Munich citizen called beer "beer", while another used the same word to speak of water: this is what the astonishing practice amounts to which the ancient Egyptians regularly followed in their language. How could anyone be blamed for shaking his head in disbelief? . . .' (Examples omitted.)

(Ibid., 7): 'In view of these and many similar cases of antithetical meaning (see the Appendix) it is beyond doubt that in one language at least there was a large number of words that denoted at once a thing and its opposite. However astonishing it may be, we are faced with the fact and have to reckon with it.'

The author goes on to reject an explanation of these circumstances which suggests that two words might happen by chance to have the same sound, and is equally firm in repudiating an attempt to refer it to the low stage of mental development in Egypt:

(Ibid., 9): 'But Egypt was anything but a home of nonsense. On the contrary, it was one of the cradles of the development of human reason. . . . It recognized a pure and dignified morality and formulated a great part of the Ten Commandments at a time when the peoples in whose hands civilization rests to-day were in the habit of slaughtering human victims as a sacrifice to bloodthirsty idols. A people that kindled the torch of justice and culture in so dark an age cannot surely have been completely stupid in everyday speech and thought. . . . Men who were able to make glass and raise and move huge blocks by machinery must at least have possessed sufficient sense not to regard a thing as being simultaneously both itself and its opposite. How are we then to reconcile this with the fact that the Egyptians allowed themselves such a strangely contradictory language? . . . that they used to give one and the same phonetic vehicle to the most mutually inimical thoughts, and used to bind together in a kind of indissoluble union things that were in the strongest opposition to each other?'

Before any explanation is attempted, mention must also be made of a further stage in this unintelligible behaviour of the Egyptian language. 'Of all the eccentricities of the Egyptian vocabulary perhaps the most extraordinary feature is that, quite apart from the words that combine antithetical meanings, it possesses other compound words in which two vocables of antithetical meanings are united so as to form a compound which bears the meaning of only one of its two constituents. Thus in this extraordinary language there are not only words meaning equally "strong" or "weak", and "command" or "obey"; but there are also compounds like "old-young", "far-near", "bind-sever", "outside-inside" . . . which, in spite of combining the extremes of difference, mean only "young", "near", "bind" and "inside" respectively So that in these compound words contradictory concepts have been quite intentionally combined, not in order to produce a third concept, as occasionally happens in Chinese, but only in order to use the compound to express the meaning of one of its contradictory parts - a part which would have had the same meaning by itself . . .'

However, the riddle is easier to solve than it appears to be. Our concepts owe their existence to comparisons. 'If it were always light we should not be able to distinguish light from dark, and consequently we should not be able to have either the concept of light or the word for it . . .' 'It is clear that everything on this planet is relative and has an independent existence only in so far as it is differentiated in respect of its relations to other things . . .' 'Since every concept is in this way the twin of its contrary, how could it be first thought of and how could it be communicated to other people who were trying to conceive it, other than by being measured against its contrary . . .' (Ibid., 15): 'Since the concept of strength could not be formed except as a contrary to weakness, the word denoting "strong" contained a simultaneous recollection of "weak", as the thing by means of which it first came into existence. In reality this word denoted neither "strong" nor "weak", but the relation and difference between the two, which created both of them equally . . .' 'Man was not in fact able to acquire his oldest and simplest concepts except as contraries to their contraries, and only learnt by degrees to separate the two sides of an antithesis and think of one without conscious comparison with the other.'

Since language serves not only to express one's own thoughts but essentially to communicate them to others the question may be raised how it was that the 'primal Egyptian' made his neighbour understand 'which side of the twin concept he meant on any particular occasion'. In the written language this was done with the help of the so-called 'determinative' signs which, placed after the alphabetical ones, assign their meaning to them and are not themselves intended to be spoken. (Ibid., 18): 'If the Egyptian word "*ken*" is to mean "strong", its sound, which is written alphabetically, is followed by the picture of an upright armed man; if the same word has to express "weak", the letters which represent the sound are followed by the picture of a squatting, limp figure. The majority of other words with two meanings are similarly accompanied by explanatory pictures.' Abel thinks that in speech the desired meaning of the spoken word was indicated by gesture.

According to Abel it is in the 'oldest roots' that antithetical double meanings are found to occur. In the subsequent course of the language's development this ambiguity disappeared and, in Ancient Egyptian at any rate, all the intermediate stages can be followed, down to the unambiguousness of modern vocabularies. 'A word that originally bore two meanings separates in the later language into two words with single meanings, in a process whereby each of the two opposed meanings takes over a particular phonetic "reduction" (modification) of the original root.' Thus, for example, in hieroglyphics the word '*ken*', 'strong-weak', already divides into '*ken*', 'strong' and '*kan*', 'weak'. 'In other words, the concepts which could only be arrived at by means of an antithesis became in course of time sufficiently familiar to men's minds to make an independent existence possible for each of their two parts and accordingly to enable a separate phonetic representative to be formed for each part.

Proof of the existence of contradictory primal meanings, which is easily established in Egyptian, extends, according to Abel, to the Semitic and Indo-European languages as well. 'How far this may happen in other language-groups remains to be seen; for although antithesis must have been present originally to the thinking minds of every race, it need not necessarily have become recognizable or have been retained everywhere in the meanings of words.'

Abel further calls attention to the fact that the philosopher Bain, apparently without knowledge that the phenomenon actually existed, claimed this double meaning of words on purely theoretical grounds as a logical necessity. The passage in question[1] begins with these sentences:

'The essential relativity of all knowledge, thought or consciousness cannot but show itself in language. If everything that we can know is viewed as a transition from something else, every experience must have two sides; and either every name must have a double meaning, or else for every meaning there must be two names.'

From the 'Appendix of Examples of Egyptian, Indo-Germanic and Arabic Antithetical Meanings' I select a few instances which may impress even those of us who are not experts in philology. In Latin '*altus*' means 'high' and 'deep', '*sacer*' 'sacred' and 'accursed'; here accordingly we have the complete antithesis in meaning without any modification of the sound of the word. Phonetic alteration to distinguish contraries is illustrated by examples like '*clamare*' ('to cry') - '*clam*' ('softly', 'secretly'); '*siccus*' ('dry') - '*succus*' ('juice'). In German '*Boden*' ['garret' or 'ground'] still means the highest as well as the lowest thing in the house. Our '*bös*' ('bad') is matched by a word '*bass*' ('good'); in Old Saxon '*bat*' ('good') corresponds to the English 'bad', and the English 'to lock' to the German '*Lücke*','*Loch*' ['hole']. We can compare the German '*kleben*' ['to stick'] with the English 'to cleave' ('to split'); the German words '*stumm*' ['dumb'] and '*Stimme*' ['voice'], and so on. In this way perhaps even the much derided derivation *lucus a non lucendo*[2] would have some sense in it.

[1] Bain (1870, 1, 54).

² [*'Lucus'* (Latin for 'a grove') is said to be derived from *'lucere'* ('to shine') because it does not shine there. (Attributed to Quintilian.)]

In his essay on 'The Origin of Language' Abel (1885, 305) calls attention to further traces of ancient difficulties in thinking. Even to-day the Englishman in order to express *'ohne'* says 'without' (*'mitohne'* ['with-without'] in German), and the East Prussian does the same. The word 'with' itself, which to-day corresponds to the German *'mit'*, originally meant 'without' as well as 'with', as can be recognized from 'withdraw and 'withhold'. The same transformation can be seen in the German *'wider'* ('against') and *'wieder'* ('together with').

For comparison with the dream-work there is another extremely strange characteristic of the ancient Egyptian language which is significant. 'In Egyptian, words can - apparently, we will say to begin with - *reverse their sound as well as their sense.* Let us suppose that the German word "*gut*" ["good"] was Egyptian: it could then mean "bad" as well as "good", and be pronounced "tug" as well as "gut". Numerous examples of such reversals of sound, which are too frequent to be explained as chance occurrences, can be produced from the Aryan and Semitic languages as well. Confining ourselves in the first instance to Germanic languages we may note: *Topf* [pot] - pot; boat - tub; wait - *täuwen* [tarry]; hurry - *Ruhe* [rest]; care - reck; *Balken* [beam] - *Klobe* [log], club. If we take

11

the other Indo-Germanic languages into consideration, the number of relevant instances grows accordingly; for example, *capere* [Latin for "take"] - *packen* [German for "seize"]; *ren* [Latin for "kidney"] - *Niere* [German for "kidney"]; leaf - *folium* [Latin for "leaf"]; *dum-a* [Russian for "thought"], *q* υμός [Greek for "spirit", "courage"] - *mêdh, mûdha* [Sanscrit for "mind"], *Mut* [German for "courage"]; *rauchen* [German for "to smoke"] - *Kur-ít* [Russian for "to smoke"]; *kreischen* [German for "to shriek"] - to shriek, etc.'

Abel tries to explain the phenomenon of reversal of sound as a doubling or reduplication of the root. Here we should find some difficulty in following the philologist. We remember in this connection how fond children are of playing at reversing the sound of words and how frequently the dream-work makes use of a reversal of the representational material for various purposes. (Here it is no longer letters but images whose order is reversed.) We should therefore be more inclined to derive reversal of sound from a factor of deeper origin.[1]

In the correspondence between the peculiarity of the dream-work mentioned at the beginning of the paper and the practice discovered by philology in the oldest languages, we may see a confirmation of the view we have formed about the regressive, archaic character of the expression of thoughts in dreams. And we psychiatrists cannot escape the suspicion that we should be better at understanding and translating the language of dreams if we knew more about the development of language.[2]

[1] For the phenomenon of reversal of sound (metathesis), which it perhaps even more intimately related to the dream-work than are contradictory meanings (antithesis), compare also Meyer-Rinteln (1909).

[2] It is plausible to suppose, too, that the original antithetical meaning of words exhibits the ready-made mechanism which is exploited for various purposes by slips of the tongue that result in the opposite being said..

www.ingramcontent.com/pod-product-compliance
Lightning Source LLC
Chambersburg PA
CBHW021622290326
41931CB00047B/1449